THE ABC'S OF PREBALLET - THE ESSENTIAL BALLET BUILDING BLOCK

A Garage Ballet Resource

DAWN C CROUCH

For my daughters, Dominique and Caroline, and all my students, PreBallet to Advanced!

———

Come visit us anytime at Garageballet.com for updates, new titles, and helpful videos.
Ballet is a lifetime asset that fosters self-esteem and confidence. Help your child be their Best!

CONTENTS

INTRODUCTION

The ABC's of PreBallet

The Essential Ballet Building Block

"It is only Perfection in the Foundations that can lead to Mastery of the Whole... Talent is Work." - Galina Ulanova

The alphabet is an essential building block of a child's education. A child must first know the twenty-six letters of the ABC's before they can use those letters to read, study, and write.

The alphabet is the core knowledge that enables reading and writing in many different languages. Other languages such as Japanese, Arabic, Russian, and Hebrew employ different symbols to write and communicate.

But make no mistake, ballet has a language all its own that in some ways surpasses the expansive influence of our own alphabet.

A student of ballet can attend and understand class anywhere in the world because the names of the steps and the structure of the class, established and organized centuries ago in the royal courts of Louis XIV (1638-1715), Le Roi Soleil, are global.

Does that mean that a student who does not have the advantage of PreBallet class will never become a dancer? Certainly Not!

———

When I was the age of PreBallet dancers, there was no such thing as a class for three to five year old children.

Why?

Because ballet training traditionally started at age six with the basic class or first level. In Europe and Russia, children were often as old as eight or nine before they began formal instruction in ballet.

Younger children often enjoyed the benefit of folk, social, or acrobatic classes within their elementary school.

I learned to square dance in elementary school and I tried to talk my mother into getting me a plaid flouncy skirt with red petticoats!

Remember the Hokey Pokey and the round dance, B-I-N-G-O? Not a bad idea using well-loved social dances to coordinate the energy and movement of young children.

I did not take my first strictly ballet class until I was eleven years old.

Rudolph Nureyev, one of the greatest male danseurs of all time, began his ballet training quite late. He was a young teenager, but he also attributed his late start to his signature bold approach to the repertoire. He was willing to push the envelope with his daring style and immersive interpretation of roles.

———

"I danced from a different angle than those who begin dancing at eight or nine. Those who have studied from the beginning never question anything."
    - Rudolph Nureyev

So, while Pre-Ballet class offers an excellent beginning for physical activity of any kind, I still maintain that a student can benefit from the study of ballet at any age... Yes, any age.

Then why send your child to PreBallet?

What are the benefits?

Early lessons in ballet, like early instruction in language development, help set the stage for the greater mental and physical enrichment of the student.

Ballet is a beautiful, mindful discipline that teaches students how to express themselves better through movement of the human body.

Ballet improves poise, self-confidence, strength, flexibility, and spatial awareness in any type of physical endeavor.

And please remember that these benefits are not about the pursuit of perfection, but instilling confidence.

Ballet elevates the body's functionality. Think of ballet as an instruction manual for movement.

Balance, Posture, and Body Alignment are the three essential keys that shape all instruction in ballet. Together, they create a lifelong skillset that ultimately becomes the greatest value of ballet training.

A dancer's body is balanced, supports decent to exceptional posture, and aligns to control focus and effort. The study of ballet imparts the ability to enjoy and enhance physicality, to live life to the fullest.

Ballet will broaden a student's horizon and serve the student well for the rest of his or her life.

"I don't mind being listed alphabetically. I do mind being treated alphabetically."
   - Maria Tallchief

A young child is like a sponge, absorbing the attention and lessons presented by their parents and teachers in a nonjudgmental and expansive mindset.

A young child watches and learns how to love, to persevere.

A young child trusts. Willing to try, a young child has not yet learned to say, "I can't."

PreBallet students are a treasure to be carefully nurtured by both teachers and parents.

This is where the importance of competent instruction takes centre stage.

A poorly taught class of any kind fosters habits and attitudes of inattention, misbehavior, and carelessness that will haunt and hamper the student for years to come.

As a parent and teacher, I want the child in my care to learn to be their best. If you're reading this book, I know you do too!

"We are what we repeatedly do. Excellence, then, is not an act but a habit." – *Aristotle*

PreBallet is the entry level class of most ballet studios. While my thoughts and advice on PreBallet are specifically targeted for PreBallet students, these basic tenets can be applied to evaluate any physical or educational endeavor.

I confess that I observe the PreBallet student through the filter of my "Ballet Helps Everything" lens.

However, the principles of "perfection in the foundation leads to the mastery of the whole" are universal, like ballet itself, to many different disciplines.

————

I grew up in New Orleans, and my teacher was Miss Lelia Haller, one of the first Americans to dance with the Paris Opera Ballet in the early 1920s.

Miss Haller was forward thinking when she founded her ballet school in the Crescent City. Within her curriculum, she developed the first PreBallet program in the city, for students age three to five.

As a young teacher with my own school, I traveled to the first teacher's conference presented by David Howard at Bard College in upstate New York.

It surprised me that Mr. Howard, the master teacher who at the time was giving private lessons to Makarova and Baryshnikov, and his associate Anne Hebard, a master teacher in her own right, devoted the lion's share of the conference content to PreBallet.

Why? Most ballet schools at the time did not even have PreBallet classes. Why the sudden attention? Why the sea change?

Ballet schools have often missed the mark on early marketing!

Capturing students early is key to student retention.

Sad to say, it is often difficult for a legitimate Ballet school to economically survive the competition of a glitter and tinsel dance studio.

————

During the height of the baby boom in the late 1950s and early 1960s, dance schools that combined ballet, tap, jazz, and acrobatics into a one hour class seized an opportunity to offer classes for young children, sometimes as early as two years old.

Once the children were established in the program, students rarely moved from their "home" school. Most were reluctant to leave all the friends that they had danced with since they were quite young.

A student who had a particular interest in ballet would have to request, beg, or in my case, be forcibly extracted by my mother, to enroll in a strictly ballet school.

There is a definite emotional component attached to the decision to change from a Dance school to a Ballet studio.

The student is often viewed as being disloyal, rather than inquisitive and searching. I have seen students remain in inferior schools and accept substandard training for years on the basis of allegiance and friendship.

————

My own beloved ballet teacher was quiet and respectful but did not particularly like it when a favorite student of hers attended a summer ballet workshop in a faraway city. The offending ballet studio? American Ballet Theatre!

————

When making the switch from a "Dance" school to a "Ballet" studio, the student is labeled as "serious," as if this is a nasty thing to be. But often, by the time this change occurs, the student may have already developed poor habits that are difficult to correct.

Think "hunt and peck" typing versus "touch" typing.

Bad habits instilled over a period of one month can take three or more months per habit to reverse.

Think about that. It's much easier to form a bad habit than a good one.

Diligence, repetition, and focused work can create new patterns of movement and alignment, but months of bad training takes years to correct.

————

I remember the "revue" programs containing quarter, half, and full page ads bought by Maw-Maw and Paw-Paw, the myriad of expensive hand sewn costumes, and the plethora of photographs, both group and individual, choreographed by professional photographers.

I remember the girl who looked like one of the hippos in Fantasia dancing toe-tap that precipitated my mother's aghast reaction and my removal from my dance school!

————

The end of year revue, a production in and of itself, is the sole and final goal of most dance schools.

Participation can be an expensive proposition for parents. Although the show is often appreciated by the audience, the student can be shortchanged on basic skills.

Ballet schools tend to be more subdued, with primary emphasis on training and technique. When a ballet is produced for an end of the year recital, each class usually performs a single ensemble class dance.

Recital programs with the names of students are often printed on one or two sheets of paper and folded in half with few, if any, ads included.

Some ballet schools do not even use costumes for recital just the regular class uniform dress of pink tights and black leotard.

If a costume is used, long white tutus are the standard. They can be reused for many years if extra fabric and several lines of hooks and eyes are placed to allow a student to grow, but not grow out of the costume.

Perhaps the long tutu is used as a base with only a Degas style ribbon of different colors at the waist, and a black velvet ribbon at the neck to complete the outfit.

Only advanced dancers wear short tutus. Wearing the iconic tutu is quite an accomplishment for a dancer. A huge milestone. Why? Because nothing is hidden by a short tutu. The position of the legs and knees are in full view.

Ballet schools emphasize basic technique and focus on training dancers to future competency, rather than preparing for a single massive year-end blowout that can last for hours and go on for several days.

———

I once knew of a dance school that sold solo, duet, and trio dances. Their Revue encompassed three separate performances over a period of three days that lasted eight to ten hours each. A total Marathon!

A ballet recital is viewed as an opportunity to display what has been learned throughout the year. A recital is an expanded observation class not an end in itself, elaborate production.

———

If a ballet school desires an active community of advanced dancers, then the PreBallet program must be developed as a deliberate part of the curriculum.

PreBallet classes filled with young students establish the foundation of a school. Crafted to excellent standards, PreBallet builds a school's credibility and reputation.

This only makes sense... PreBallet is the logical base of a school's pyramid of classes because student advancement and retention are primary goals.

The number of PreBallet classes should be roughly double the number of advanced classes.

If a school offers advanced class every day of the week but Sunday, then the school should strive to schedule twelve PreBallet classes.

Throughout the years it takes for a student to progress from PreBallet to Advanced, a certain number of students will leave the school. Some will move away to a different city, others will leave to pursue the myriad of other activities that are available to children in our society today, and some students may be forced to quit due to personal circumstances.

Attrition averages about twenty to forty percent each season throughout the industry.

Chapter One

FUN OR INSTRUCTION?

"Children are great imitators. So, give them something great to imitate." - *Anonymous*

THERE IS one last argument that keeps parents from enrolling their child in a Ballet school's PreBallet program and it's an insidious one. Very sneaky and underhanded, but I've heard it a million times.

"I just want my child to have FUN!"

Many parents enroll their child in a dance school rather than a ballet school because they have the mistaken notion that a PreBallet class with the underpinnings of ballet training is more serious and therefore less fun.

This could not be farther from the truth!

I have literally taught hundreds of children in PreBallet and believe me, my class is the most fun class in the entire world!

Why? Because this is a monkey see, monkey do class!

In PreBallet class, I dance the whole thing! Standing up, getting down on the floor, running on half-pointe, tracing the pattern of a ronde de jambe, jumping like a bunny rabbit... You get the idea!

If I stop, the students stop too. As we dance together, a connection forms between the students and the teacher, as if my efforts command and direct the young students' movement as well.

"Children see magic because they look for it." - *Christopher Moore*

PreBallet is by far the most physical of all the classes I teach. In advanced class, I offer suggestions and analysis to coach a better performance from a trained dancer. In basic and intermediate class, I may demonstrate a combination or exercise, but the value of my expertise is in analyzing and correcting the quality of the student's combination.

PreBallet students follow the movement of the teacher. If I perform a step incorrectly, then they will.

If a teacher is sitting in a chair barking orders, what good is that? If the teacher is not dancing, then there is nothing for the student to imitate.

"One has to have a talent for teaching, a separate talent, different from the kind that makes a great performer."
    - *Alexandra Danilova*

———

I had the privilege of studying with Madame Danilova during a summer sojourn in New York when I was fifteen. Madame's classes were quite popular, such a draw that there were often too many students to fit in the studio. There literally was no place to stand, much less take barre and dance centre.

So... Everyone had to audition to take the class. How?

Madame started with double pirouettes. That simple exercise alone usually eliminated enough students to begin class with a more reasonable number.

What did she look for? The finish. A lot of dancers can perform a double turn; not so many can finish up, then close to a fifth position. Amazing, but true.

Yes, I made the cut, and I have always tried to emulate her insight and ability to target little corrections that would lead to big improvements.

A contemporary of George Balanchine, Alexandra Danilova received her early training at the Russian Imperial Ballet School in St. Petersburg and escaped to the west with Balanchine after the Bolshevik Revolution.

Although she was a prima ballerina with Diaghilev's Ballet Russe de Monte Carlo, Madame Danilova is primarily respected and remembered for her teaching and coaching abilities.

She is immortalized in a cameo role where she played herself coaching the young soloist in the 1977 movie The Turning Point starring Leslie Browne and Mikhail Baryshnikov.

Danilova is a great example of someone who was a teacher more than a dancer.

————

I believe the best teacher for PreBallet is patient and plays along with her PreBallet students, coaxing them with a gentle, quiet hand through miracles and mistakes.

PreBallet class should be nonstop, from warm-up to a moderated barre, to centre dances. All performed with a smile and a certain amount of magic!

————

In 1995, I was teaching at Community Ballet which is now known as Huntsville Ballet in Huntsville, AL. The largest studio was located in half of the gym of a former high school.

This was a particularly fun place to dance a PreBallet class. Lower level classes are usually consigned to the smaller studios to corral the children better, but I loved the expanse of half of a gym because of the freedom of movement that the space allowed.

That year, one of my PreBallet students was completely deaf.

The young lady was on the high side of PreBallet age, five years old. This is very close to six years old which is, of course, the age that most students move into basic class.

She had never taken ballet before, and her mother thought that it would be better to begin in the PreBallet section.

This young girl could feel the vibration of the music through the sprung floor of the studio.

A "sprung" floor is a wooden floor or a raised floor. The surface that the dancers use does not make direct contact with the cement underlayer and is covered on top with vinyl ballet flooring. Because there is a certain "give" in the floor, a "sprung" floor protects the dancers' joints and tendons.

Dancing directly on a concrete floor in a studio is a big red flag. Never allow a young dancer, or a dancer of any age or any level to dance consistently on concrete.

My young student was naturally rhythmic and attuned to the "beat" of the music. More than that, this young girl focused on my movement with an intensity that I truly have never experienced before or since.

If I had done a double tour en l'air, she would have given it her best shot to duplicate my lead.

She was a joy to teach and a real asset to the class. The younger dancers acted as guardian and mentor to her, gently touching her arm when the flow of the dance was about to change.

About that same time, Miss Alabama Heather Whitestone was crowned Miss America.

When Miss Whitestone was a toddler, she lost her hearing due to a severe ear infection. She was the first deaf Miss America and she happened to be an excellent ballet dancer. A perfect combination.

When I heard that Miss Whitestone was going to visit Huntsville, I made inquiries.

A gracious and kind person, Miss Whitestone altered her busy schedule and arranged a meeting with my young deaf student and her mother.

Her poise and generosity really made a difference to this entire family!

The young student continued her training and became a good dancer... All by imitation!

———

Chapter Two

A IS FOR ALIGNMENT, ASSURANCE, AND ATTITUDE

"Minor things can become moments of great revelation when encountered for the first time."

- Margot Fonteyn

PREBALLET SHOULD BE joyous and gratifying for the young student with the discipline and seriousness of the undertaking well hidden in the structure of the class.

This alignment of priorities establishes a framework for the exercises and dances conducted during class.

How your child is welcomed, supervised within the class, and returned to your care is of upmost importance. A child unencumbered by doubt, worry, and separation anxiety, can focus on learning and enjoy to the fullest the opportunity offered to them.

As the entry level, PreBallet class serves as the introduction to, and first experience of the student with ballet. This may be one of the first times that the child is leaving her mother, father, or caregiver, a big step for a three to five year old.

At the beginning of class, the teacher should present as welcoming and friendly, to create an atmosphere of inclusion and ease. As a teacher, I ask a lot of the child. I request their trust.

As the child enters the studio, the parent should leave.

The child has stepped into a different world where he or she has become a student who will be asked to try new and different things.

A PreBallet student cannot focus on the teacher and the parent at the same time.

As a parent, if you feel comfortable with the safety and ambiance of the studio then commit to turning away and entrust your child with the teacher.

If your child balks, you may sit with them at the door into the studio but do try to project a confident outlook that the class will be worthwhile.

Do not enter the spatial boundary of the class.

A child should enter the studio voluntarily.

Sometimes a moment or two of watching the start of the class with the parent at the doorway as it begins is all it takes to persuade the child to join in the circle.

Occasionally, I will offer my hand to the child and accompany them to the centre circle, but I never physically hold a child or pull them into the class against their will.

I expect the parent to leave as soon as the child makes the decision to take the class. Parent and teacher must work together to encourage the child to take that first step toward independence.

I take the responsibility of my PreBallet charges very seriously.

Once the student is in my care, they do not leave my sight until the parent or caregiver picks them up at the door of the studio, unless they are escorted to the restroom by my trained helper.

Note I did not say that my care ends at the Fini of class, nor do I leave the students to go wait in the reception area with older students or other parents.

I physically hand off the PreBallet student to the parent that dropped them off for class, or the designated caregiver.

If the parent or caregiver is late picking up the child, then the student stays in the studio with me until I see the designated parent or caregiver at the door.

In this day and time, I will take no chances with a child's safety and well-being. None.

———

Helpers in my PreBallet class are chosen from a list of my more advanced dancers. I have usually worked with these dancers for several years and know them well. I've even had Helpers who I've trained since they were my students in PreBallet.

I expect my Helpers to dance the class as if they are one of the young students.

Helpers should not correct, talk, lift a student, hold a student in their lap, or otherwise distract from the main person the students should be watching... the Teacher.

Too much interaction with Helpers disturbs the flow of the class.

There are two main reasons for allowing an older student to help in class.

The first is to teach the revered tradition of ballet, teacher to student, by taking the class and building the muscle memory by performing the steps.

The second reason is to personally escort students to the restroom, if the need arises. Restroom breaks should be allowed by necessity only, and one student at a time.

Very few of students try to dodge the class when they realize that they are accompanied, and immediately returned after, necessities are taken care of.

I never have more than two Helpers for a PreBallet class.

———

In consideration of the care and individual attention given each student in class, I believe that class size should range from a minimum of six students to a maximum of twelve students.

Why a minimum?

The dynamic of class depends on the connection between the teacher and a number of students. Six students allow for a group mentality to develop, which fosters unified cooperation and establishes positive peer pressure.

In a group of six students, a healthy collaborative teamwork ensures that the class stays motivated and continues to move forward. Also, if a student is absent, there are still enough students to proceed.

Why a maximum?

While many studios are tempted to pack PreBallet classes, a group of more than twelve students this age can be controlled but will not receive the amount of individual attention necessary for appropriate praise and correction.

That individual response is especially important to motivate and support beginning efforts.

In advanced class, a student can go weeks without hearing praise or correction from their teacher. Not in my class, but in many. Class size often tops thirty.

I remember in my Intermediate class when I was eleven, we had six lines of five to eight students in each line and worked in groups during centre exercises. I had to perform a step exceptionally well to get a personal comment from my teacher, but I also had dancers that were well trained and above my level to follow.

PreBallet is personal.

While a minimum number of students establishes a group dynamic, a maximum number ensures students will receive individual care and concern.

"Even the smallest person can change the course of the future."
  - Lady Galadriel, Lord of the Rings

What about the length of the class?

I have taught PreBallet in studios where the class length was forty-five minutes. This is usually done as a concession to teaching needs.

At forty-five minutes, a second PreBallet class immediately follows the first. Both classes last an hour and a half in consideration of the teacher who often has a basic class and then either Intermediate/Advanced, Advanced, or Company class right after. These upper level classes are usually an hour and a half to two hours long each.

A full evening of teaching to be sure!

I prefer a one hour PreBallet class because the pace is smoother and allows for extra games and stretches.

Also, parents prefer an hour class because they can actually leave the premises, run an errand, and return on time.

Forty-five minutes is pushing the envelope for leaving the studio, especially when the parent or caregiver must hand deliver the student and personally pick them up within the building.

The shorter class also tempts the parent to remain in the reception area to try to observe, which I do not recommend.

About halfway through the Fall semester, I extend an invitation to parents, grandparents, and siblings to attend a planned observation class.

By that time, the pattern of the class is firmly established, and the students are proud to display their accomplishments.

———

I always time my PreBallet Fall semester observation class to coincide with Halloween. This class isn't really about observation since I ask parents to participate and take the class with their child.

Everyone dresses in Halloween costumes. My only rule is that costumes allow freedom of movement and do not pose a risk for falling.

Most of the time, mothers and sometimes fathers, attend, perhaps with a younger sibling.

By actually taking the class, parents understand in a very visceral way that the class involves a lot of movement, listening, and awareness.

Before I begin, I always caution my young students that it is up to them to make sure that their parents behave and follow the rules of the class.

They love having the shoe on the other foot, and I've seen very small little dancers telling their daddy that he is not trying hard enough and to please follow directions!

Once, I remember a class that included a mother who worked as anchor for the local news channel and was a bit of a celebrity.

She showed up with a camera crew!

I promise, cross my heart, that I knew nothing of this development until it happened.

Another mother in the class happened to be wearing a zebra print leotard. Hmmm...

Don't ever wear something that you wouldn't want to be seen in on the evening news! Good advice for anyone!

———

Chapter Three

B IS FOR BALLERINAS AND BALANCE

"Dance is bigger than the physical body. When you extend your arm, it doesn't stop at the end of your fingers, because you're dancing bigger than that: you're dancing spirit."
 - Judith Jamison

PreBallet class is a total Move-A-Thon! As in, Let's Get Going!

Now, I know this seems self-evident, but I have seen many different PreBallet classes over the years based solely on corralling and controlling the students, thereby inhibiting movement.

The object of the class seems to be keeping the children pinned to a single location for great lengths of time.

One of my pet peeves is when a studio sets eight to ten inch plastic dots on the floor, then expects a student to stand on them for great lengths of time.

I have never seen an Intermediate or Advanced student standing on an orange or purple dot!

Why do Teachers and Helpers admonish students to stand on a plastic dot?

To maintain order and control of the class.

The unintended consequence is that standing on a dot inhibits movement.

I use other tactics.

There are two important strategies I use in my PreBallet class to command and direct the flow of movement.

The first order of business in my class, as I sit in a circle at the center of the studio with my students, is to make sure that I not only know each student's name but that I am pronouncing it correctly.

I cannot emphasize enough the importance of this gesture.

I start every single class by going over the students' names from mid-August all the way to early June and recital.

Why is this so important?

"Attention is the rarest and purest form of generosity."
   - Simone Weil

When I give a correction, praise, ask someone to stand in line, or be the leader of the line, I say their name first, then whatever I say after is more effective.

Once the class starts, I often call names to identify the student before I ask that they perform an exercise.

There are sci-fi novels that use this concept!

Knowing someone's name gives you a certain degree of power and authority over them, in a good way, and also allows you to recognize that individual person.

Sounds mysterious... Doesn't it?

But let's look at how this works. Think about how it encourages for the better. "Well Done!" Or "Emily, great job!"

Think of it the opposite way: "Stop running. Be quiet." Or "Brian, stay still now." Yip, works every time...

Now the funny thing is, I never remember adult names. Perhaps because I am a child at heart.

I will remember a student's name for years, but a parent will always be Sarah's mother or Austin's dad. Oh well...

———

In my early years of teaching, I had a once in a lifetime experience with names in a PreBallet class. I taught it early on a Thursday morning, my longest day in the week.

When I first started teaching, I was a sophomore in college and I actually paid for my tuition, books, car, and gas, with the money I earned teaching ballet classes. That would be impossible now, but I managed then.

That spring semester, I carried fifteen hours of an academic course load. In addition, on Thursdays, I taught two PreBallet, one Child's basic, and two Adult basic classes for a total of five and a half hours of studio time.

I would teach a PreBallet and Adult Basic in the morning then go to my academic classes, and finally return to the studio for the evening schedule.

I've never had a class like my early morning Thursday PreBallet before or since.

Within the twelve students, there were three sets of twins and everyone in the class was either named Jessica or Heather! Crazy!

I finally resorted to getting everyone different colored bows for the buns in their hair so there was Blue Heather and Green Heather, a Red Jessica and Lavender Jessica, etc.

The kids seemed to like it, and we were all on named individual standing again. Although I did think it was pretty easy to say either Heather or Jessica and have half the class turn and look!

———

"Children will listen to you after they feel listened to."
  - Jane Nelson

The next order of business in my PreBallet class is that I teach students the concept of Jump-Sit.

Now, this isn't a ballet step. A Jump-Sit is exactly what it sounds like: I start in a standing position, jump up enough to cross my ankles, then landing first on the ball of my foot, drop to the ground and sit cross legged.

The hands cannot be used on the way down in a Jump-Sit. Once seated, the student is expected to sit tall, with as straight a back as possible, good posture, with the hands folded in his or her lap.

We practice Jump-Sit quite a bit since it is a little trickier than it sounds but Jump-Sit is important for several reasons.

The Jump-Sit requires thought and coordination to execute. Jumping up and coming down to a cross legged sit on the floor is difficult enough, requiring both focus and concentration.

Those qualities are important to a dancer and a successful class.

We practice Jump-Sit as a group, then individually. If someone has trouble, the class gives encouragement, and the student tries one additional time.

This skill is not to devolve into a bone of contention. I have never had a student that didn't eventually get the Jump-Sit combination.

A second reason Jump-Sit is useful in the PreBallet environment is because it acts as a reset button.

Whenever and wherever I as a teacher say, "Jump-Sit," the class stops what they are doing and does the step.

Jump-Sit stops the action, gives a rest, and allows the teacher to regroup before moving to the next exercise.

I don't know if classroom grade schoolteachers do this anymore, but I know of several teachers who would use a clap sequence or turn off the overhead lights when the class was getting unruly, talking too much, or moving around in a disorganized fashion.

These simple unspoken cautions immediately got everyone's attention. The class innately understood that the reason the teacher did this was to restore order and refocus the class.

Jump-Sit is a behavioral tool, as well as a valuable physical exercise. The children like to perform the exercise and are proud of their accomplishment when they achieve the Jump-Sit without landing on their bottom or falling to the side.

They sit straight and tall and I always comment how happy I am that they have conquered the difficult drill. Because it is difficult... Do you think you can do it? Give it a try.

With Jump-Sit and name recognition on the way to mastery, the rest of our allotted time is well-filled and purposeful.

I will offer a sample class in a later chapter, but effort and direction are the hallmark of any good PreBallet class, and the very reason why PreBallet is the most physically demanding of all the classes I teach.

We run, jump, use our arms and keep the tempo throughout the entire class.

There is no time for "free dance" or any other unchoreographed, spontaneous material.

Your little student can "free dance" at home, and they probably do which is one of the reasons you thought that ballet class might be enjoyable to begin with.

"Jumping for Joy if a very basic human reaction, and a child skipping down the street is simply an untrained dancer." - Margot Fonteyn

It is the duty of a PreBallet teacher to conduct a meaningful class, not to sit and watch untrained dancers move about like they do at home.

I love at home dance parties as much as any other mom, sister, and friend, but the parents of my students are paying for my knowledge and expertise, not for a larger space to play.

Which leads me to my final point about the tempo and physicality of the PreBallet class.

Who is teaching the class?

I firmly believe that the director of the studio, or at least one of the senior faculty, should teach at least one PreBallet class per week.

This is valuable for the teachers too, if only to have an accurate view on the level of training and how the students are responding to the class.

I am not necessarily suspect of new or young teachers. PreBallet classes were some of the first classes I taught for Miss Haller.

But a question that should be asked is... Are the classes standardized within the studio, or at least following some pre-set curriculum or guidelines? Or is the "new" teacher just winging it?

Remember, a studio is known by the dancers they create, and the dancers they intend to develop begin in PreBallet. Not all, but most.

If PreBallet classes have no standards and no specific goals, how can your young dancer hope to exhibit a standard of excellence?

A PreBallet class should be treated with respect, and with the intention that this class is the foundation of the studio, not a cash cow placeholder to be taught by any warm body calling themselves a teacher.

Prevailing expectations should apply. If the teacher is inexperienced, then she should at least be well prepared, and given a standard class or list of exercises to include in her class, with the directive to follow them to the letter.

As a parent, you are paying for professional and meaningful instruction not an hour of babysitting.

Chapter Four

C IS FOR CHASSÉ, CONSISTENCY, AND CORPS DE BALLET

"A real ballerina must fill her space with her own personality." - *Natalia Makarova*

I TOTALLY AGREE with Natalia Makarova, who when she won the top award for dance education from Dance Magazine, was quoted as saying that her husband didn't help her very much, but at least he stayed out of her way.

If a real ballerina has any hope of filling her space with her own special personality, then she must first understand the boundaries of her space, which leads to the crucial concept of Spatial Awareness.

Spatial Awareness is a lifelong pursuit because the ability to appreciate the location of your body (and later, vehicle) in relation to other people or nearby objects will go a long way to ensure your safety, security, and general well-being.

PreBallet class helps the young student grasp the ideas of direction and distance.

This applies not only with respect to their individual limits of place, but their individual separateness.

At this young age, children are still very close to the infantile notion that they and their parents are one interconnected being.

Spatial awareness is key to protection and defense. Think of a young child riding a bike but looking at a little sister waving from her buggy. He or she might crash into a parked car, the garbage can, or worse, inadvertently ride the bike into the street.

How can youngsters know they are about to fall or slip if they aren't sure where they stand? Or where they are in relation to the edge between a pond and terra firma?

PreBallet class also incorporates the beginnings of the mindfulness exhibited in the Corps de Ballet, central to all classical choreography.

Dancers move as a group, as well as move within the group by changing lines, taking turns, running in concentric circles, and pretending to pick flowers for sweet mothers in a pretend beautiful garden.

PreBallet class rehearses tons of Ballet Runs.

A Ballet Run is when a dancer rises to the ball of their foot on half-pointe and moves their feet very fast while still preserving their balance by keeping their feet directly beneath them.

Sounds easy, huh?

A Ballet Run in no way resembles a "we are playing chase in the backyard run."

First, the steps taken are on half-pointe and the feet are kept close together, as close to first position as possible, and the feet stay underneath the body.

In a full out fifty yard dash run, the balance pointe of the body is ahead of the temporal space of the running body.

Think of the end of an Olympic race.

The final push of the athlete throws the momentum of the balance point forward.

As the winner crosses the finish line, the runner often has to flail their arms and struggle to stay upright and not fall since their balance point is far ahead of their body.

And that is not the only thing a PreBallet student has to think about during a Ballet Run. Feet are fast, but they are also supposed to be super quiet.

The audience should not hear clodhopper feet slapping the stage floor.

Big No-No!

Fast and quiet feet is a must. Many of the centre dances of PreBallet incorporate Ballet Runs of the entire "Corps de Ballet" of students upstage, downstage, stage right and stage left.

Are the students in line? LOL! Absolutely not!

They often look like a swarm of bees, each running at their own pace. In the early weeks of class, the students often race to be the first to get to the front, side, or back.

The teacher should discourage racing, and also should refrain from ever calling on the first person to arrive at the destination.

Do students crash into each other or the wall? Occasionally... But that is another graphic lesson in spatial awareness.

The Ballet Run requires fast and quiet feet while using both eyes to look straight ahead the entire time.

Look forward. Look where you are running. Look to the space your body will occupy in the near future.

This way, the dancer becomes cognizant of their space and protects it by anticipating the obstacles ahead and around them. Perhaps another dancer. The wall. A mirror...

Anticipating next moves is a worthy ambition for any person because reading the flow of an activity adds to the potential for success.

Whether in Ballet, Chess, or planning which college to attend, anticipating next moves is an important life skill.

These early dances in PreBallet teach the need for teamwork, for respect of another dancer's space, and for flexible spontaneity that allows for a mid-course correction.

"You're never more of an individual than when you're a happy team player."
- Suzanne Farrell

If a PreBallet student can adjust and avoid a crash in the studio, then they will also be more aware of their surroundings outside of the studio.

By practicing spatial awareness, they learn to notice details.

Because they work as a group, the PreBallet class will help each other endure. They will run longer and faster in a group than if they practice the same run individually.

When teaching basic, intermediate, and advanced classes, I expect students to hold their place in line, know how to properly change lines, and rotate groups at the end or beginning of an exercise.

The older dancers know how to move across the floor in any direction, front, back or diagonally, with poised confidence.

In Pre-Ballet class, I teach the concept of the Ballet Run with fast, quiet feet and looking directly ahead.

Then I say a little prayer for no train wrecks.

But I still trust the students to discover their own physical limits, and to keep a safe distance from each other as they dance.

Back to my pet peeve of studios that use eight to ten inch plastic dots to achieve a straight line!

If I've done my job correctly, the children know how to line up and maintain a reasonably straight line. It may not be a Rockette line, but they are not getting paid for that professional level of straightness.

If they were getting paid, I'd coach them until the line was perfect and we would all get paid!

I do not expect straight lines in PreBallet. No one should. It's not that important at this age.

What should be visible in a PreBallet class is a reasonable attempt at lines, big circles, little circles, and a great deal of Move-A-Thon!

"Dancing is more than moving body parts; it is a pathway of expressing your deepest inner thoughts." - Normani Kordei

———

If one of the aims of ballet instruction is individual expression, then why would I want to stifle and constrict the natural current of the dancer?

I want to harness the energy and enthusiasm, not train it out of the student.

Ballet is all about the wordless communication of our inner emotions.

I remember one PreBallet class where I pretend along with my students that we have fallen into a magical sleep and awaken to a lush garden full of flowers. We use our Ballet Run to move through the studio and pick flowers for a bouquet for our mothers.

My own heart was a little heavy that day because my mother had passed the week before. I tried to concentrate and focus on picking the most beautiful bouquet I could.

At the end of the dance, we did our Jump-Sit in a circle and sat around a small pond. We filled our pretend vases with water and carefully placed our flowers in the vases.

One little girl was being particularly careful in placing the flowers. As she fixed her vase, she named each color and type of flower: a rose, a daisy.

I remember glancing at the clock because I don't like to linger and try to keep the forward momentum steady and strong throughout the class.

I asked if she was finished. She said almost. The clock ticked on.

I was about to overrule her and move on to the next dance, when she said, "My flowers this week are for my brother."

I replied that it was fine to give the flowers to her brother if she wanted to, then she looked up at me and said, "He's in heaven now."

The dance indeed articulated her deepest thoughts.

———

"Dance is the purest expression of every emotion, earthly and spiritual." - Anna Pavlova

My last comment on spatial awareness is about how the teacher physically presents the material to the class.

In upper level ballet classes, basic, intermediate, and advanced, I face the students directly which means that any step or combination I demonstrate is performed as a mirror image of what I want the students to perform.

If I say begin with your right hand, I start with my left and so on. I am acting as a mirror image of the students. The older students respond best face to face, when spoken to directly, but PreBallet students are a little different.

PreBallet seems to work best when the teacher faces the same direction as the little students.

PreBallet students tend to look into the mirror and regard the tableau as a whole so when I teach PreBallet, I face the mirror and become a part of the class. I'm just a little taller and a little heavier!

Spatial awareness is an important concept in the success of any physical endeavor, sport, dance, or simply receiving an award on stage, or entering an office for an interview.

Is it too early to consider the importance of spatial awareness in situations like this?

No, it's never too early to develop skill and talent.

"To give anything less than your best is to sacrifice the gift." - Steve Roland Prefontaine

Chapter Five

D IS FOR DISCIPLINE, E IS FOR ETIQUETTE, EFFORT AND F IS FOR FOCUS

"Learning ballet is wonderful for children even if they never become dancers. It is wonderful because it teaches discipline, grace, and manners." - Anna Paskevska

BALLET IS AS MUCH a world treasure as each UNESCO World Heritage site of historically significant buildings and places.

The structure and manners of the class preserved by Ballet Etiquette embrace the art's global philosophy and ensure the continuance of the centuries old tradition.

PreBallet is not exempt from the cultural mores of Ballet Discipline or Etiquette, but rather the first invitation to the world of beauty and custom.

In practical terms, what does the observance of ballet etiquette contribute to the class?

When you consider enrolling your child in a studio, go to observe a PreBallet class, or participate in your child's class, there is one question that you should ask.

Does the teacher maintain order in their class?

If the class looks like chaos, then all bets are off. Your child may learn something but not what you intended...

I never raise my voice in class. That is a completely useless endeavor.

In fact, as anyone who has ever taken class with me knows that I become completely silent if I observe extraneous talking, unruly behavior, or impolite exchanges between students.

I stand and look. I may even smile.

Silence tends to radiate.

My quiet expands in circles like a rock hitting the surface of a still lake, until the one or two students engaging in the inappropriate behavior become isolated within the silence.

This happens in every level class, PreBallet to Advanced, that I teach, and it doesn't happen often.

When you send your child to ballet class, you should expect a professional atmosphere, a focused zone of concentration that allows the beauty of the music and the art form to shine.

Another important point is that a teacher who commands her class leaves no room for bullying within the class.

A fellow student or an older helper should never comment or offer any correction to another student, good or bad. This is completely inappropriate.

Each student should only be concerned with their own performance of a step or combination.

Comments and corrections on performance are the teacher's prerogative and job.

What aspects of Ballet Etiquette are introduced in PreBallet?

Class is class, whatever level, however many are in the class. All attention should be focused on the teacher and performing the steps, combinations, and dances.

Class is not a place for conversation about off topic subjects.

I understand that sometimes off topic subjects will creep into the class, but that should be the rare exception.

If a student is under extreme duress, I, as the teacher, should acknowledge and deal with the situation in the moment.

———

Death and divorce are the two unavoidable topics that may rise to the surface in an otherwise regular ballet class. These two subjects are both extreme and traumatic.

Whether PreBallet or Advanced, the student should be treated with kindness and sincere consolation. The PreBallet student whose brother passed. An advanced student whose father was so happy to get a job painting commercial buildings then fell to his death. A mother or father's unexpected car wreck or heart attack.

Many times, the adults in these student's lives are so overwhelmed that they send the children to class in a desperate plea for support.

What I have seen is that the student continues to work hard. They take class. They dance.

Why?

Because Ballet focuses the mind as well as the body.

When you take a class – whether you are an adult, a teen, a child, or a PreBallet student, - you become part of a training tradition that both transcends yet is totally involved in the present and looking forward.

You dance with all the incredible dancers of the past and you dance to ensure the future.

Simply stated, the show must go on...

———

"Dance is the movement of the universe concentrated in an individual."
   - Isadora Duncan

Ballet helps a person live in the present.

Conversation about what a student had for breakfast; the new toy Grandma bought; what they want for Christmas; or the ticket dad or mom got when they were speeding, should not be allowed in class. No need to point it out, but a teacher should smile and redirect.

Keep on target. Keep the focus of the class clear.

How can extraneous conversation be best avoided?

Keep the class moving!

It's hard to talk when you are trying to breathe!

One of the special skills required of a teacher is that she must be able to explain an exercise while demonstrating the step!

If there are too many lulls between exercises, the students will fill the void. The teacher's responsibility is to plan ahead and keep the energy of the class pressing onward.

The essence of ballet, of dance of any kind, is to express emotion and passion without words. Never let conversation get in the way of that purpose. We are in class to dance not have a conversation.

"Words can distance a dancer from the music and from her own impulses, and make her movement appear remote and flat." - *Jennifer Homans*

The final bow is central to Ballet Etiquette. Remember your Jane Austen! I can still picture Lizzie and Darcy bowing to each other! Awesome!

When two people meet, gentlemen bow and the ladies curtsy. In these days, a touchless bow and curtsy may be revived. But in ballet class, the bow and curtsy never left!

When entering the class, a PreBallet student proceeds straight to their Jump-Sit in the centre circle. All other level classes go to the barre.

But every ballet class, no matter the level, ends the same...

The teacher and students bow to each other.

The bow (and here I include curtsy within the broader term "bow") is a gesture of gratitude and respect between the students and the teacher.

I repeat... Every ballet class should end with a bow.

I have worked at studios that take this one step farther. Along with a general bow between the class and the teacher at the immediate end of the class, each individual student bows to the teacher and verbally thanks them for class before they exit the studio. Nice!

Students and teachers bow in this day and time?

Yes, every time I teach class.

———

My youngest son is married to a young lady from Sweden. Once when visiting for Thanksgiving, they came to observe class at the studio.

I thought the students would benefit from meeting someone from a different country. Martha is not a dancer, but she is an awesome skier!

I have to admit that my students treated Martha as if she was an elf straight out of Lord of the Rings! She does have the look. They kept asking her to talk because they were totally fascinated with her beautiful accent.

But my son, who was never known for hanging out with me at the ballet studio, noticed something else.

The next morning, he helped me prepare the turkey for the oven and randomly said, "Those kids bowed to you. They hung on every word you said, and they bowed."

I replied that my students did that all the time, that I expected it of them, and I explained that this was proper class procedure. He was impressed. Wow!

———

In Pre-Ballet class, I use the final curtsy with female students and bow for male students as the last exercise before they leave the studio.

I open the door to the studio, and the parents or guardians are waiting outside because as I've explained, I require a physical handoff for each child.

Instead of a grand rush to the door, each student maintains their Jump-Sit position, remembering good posture, back straight and hands folded in lap.

By the end of the class, this is the last thing the student wants to do. They want to run to their mom or dad and tell them what they've done in class.

But this exercise of waiting for their turn helps reinforce self-control and the habit of discipline established in the class.

Calling on each student individually, I expect them to execute a Ballet Run, fast and quiet feet, to meet me at the door.

I hold hands with each student to provide a steady balance, and as a mirror image, I tendu to second with my right leg as they tendu to second with their left leg.

We then bend our knee and bring our pointed foot to the back to curtsy. This is not as easy as it sounds, but an ending gesture of appreciation and value is part of the custom of the ballet class. A curtsy or bow is a step that must be practiced.

Taking turns, entering class in a quiet manner, no unnecessary conversation, and always ending class with a bow are just some of the customary behavior expected in any credible ballet class.

When observing classes and evaluating a studio, make sure class etiquette is not only present but faithfully followed.

Chapter Six

G IS FOR GRANDE AND J FOR JAMBE... M IS FOR MORES AND ALL THINGS BEYOND

"Dancers are made, not born."
- Mikhail Baryshnikov

FRENCH WAS the language of the day during the reign of Louis IX, Le Roi Soleil, which lasted from 1638 to 1715 so the initially codified steps were naturally given French names.

Plié, Tendu, Ronde de Jambe...

French terminology and the structure of the ballet class combine to create a universal language that enables a student of ballet to travel the globe with an ability to understand and participate in class.

Ballet class provides a common thread, and immediately offers a source of friendship in foreign places.

So, forget about calling Pliés "knee bends" or Battement Cloches "swing swangs." That just will not cut it!

I'll take this one step further.

As I teach PreBallet students, I use this unique opportunity to introduce them not only to ballet terms, but also to a different language along the way.

I often include simple commands and instructions en Français.

Just phrases and words that teachers might normally say in class such as Écoutez or "listen," Silencieuse or "quiet," Maintenant or "now," and Rapidement or "vite." I often say vite very quickly while clapping my hands, "Vite ! Vite ! Fast ! Hurry !"

Est-ce que tu comprends ce que j'ai dit ?

PreBallet students respond well to a foreign language.

Speaking French as a normal part of class encourages them to listen closely, and to think about what they are asked to do.

If they don't understand what I have just said, they will always let me know.

I introduce ballet terminology during the abbreviated ballet barre so that the terms become a normal part of their vocabulary.

This association becomes ingrained, just as whenever a student performs a step, that step is further incorporated into their muscle memory.

For PreBallet the terms include Plié, Relevé, Tendu, and Grande Battement. I translate the French names to English, then return to the French.

I also familiarize the students with oppositions such as Petit which means "little," and Grande which is, of course, "big," as well as names for parts of the body - la tête for the head; les épaules for shoulders; les bras for arms; les jambes for legs; les mains for hands; les pied for feet, and so on.

The proper name for the step must be associated with the step itself for the connection to have a lasting benefit.

The whole purpose of using proper terminology is to prepare a dancer for interaction within the global community.

If a teacher uses no terminology, English equivalents, or incorrect nicknames, a big red flag should run up the pole.

Now, I'm not saying that the teacher is a total fraud if she doesn't teach correct French terminology, but it will make your child's future life as a dancer more difficult.

———

When I was a teenager, I once attended a series of master classes at the Fairmont Roosevelt Hotel with Vincenzo Celli who studied with Cecchetti, one of the great legends of Ballet.

A group of dancers from Algiers, Louisiana, which is located just across the river from New Orleans, also took the workshop.

The teacher from their home school was a total Yat! Sorry, you'll have to be from the ninth ward in New Orleans to understand the reference.

This particular Teacher from Algiers called pirouettes spins, Grande Battements were high kicks, and Frappes were known as strike outs.

Her dancers were well trained and could perform the steps impeccably, but they were at a disadvantage.

Master Celli, who was elderly and carried a cane with a cobra head carved into the top, conducted the master class from a chair at the front of the conference hall.

No biggie.

He offered corrections and advice in English, but he used the French terminology for all exercises to be performed.

The students from Algiers were at a complete loss at what to do.

Although they were good dancers, they could not translate his words into a combination of the steps.

Sad to watch, they marked the exercise behind other often inferior dancers only because they didn't know the names of the steps.

———

Even in PreBallet, a Plié is a Plié.

What if you as a parent had pet words for every noun in the household? How could the child function when they attend school?

French terminology and ballet are all part of the same set, a unified package like a horse a bridle, and a saddle all working together to allow a person to ride.

"To be who you are and become what you are capable of is the only goal worth living."

- Alvin Ailey

Let's add music to this totality.

Be clear about one point. PreBallet does not equal Disney. While I never use Disney music in class unless it was first based on a classical piece (ex. *Once Upon a Dream from Sleeping Beauty)*, I do employ any music that I feel has the power to inspire and energize the students.

I use music from *Pirates of the Caribbean, Lord of the Rings,* and even a Dolly Parton song or two at Christmas. I just love *Two Step 'round the Christmas Tree* by Suzy Bogguss. The quick tempo of that song really smokes!

In PreBallet, I dance special Christmas classes during the month of December, making sure to have a few Hanukkah songs in the mix. *Frosty the Snowman* is a favorite, but I also use other classic pieces from *Les Patineurs* (The Skaters), by Meyerbeer.

All my PreBallet students learn a PreBallet version of the *Nutcracker's Sugar Plum*.

If any boys are in the class, I include the *Russian Variation from Nutcracker* as well.

But special occasion music should be a diversion, a treat.

Class music should always seek a firm basis in the classical repertoire written for ballet and opera.

Ask yourself. When will children have the opportunity to be exposed to some of the best music the world has ever produced? Not many instances.

Just as with the correct French terminology, children deserve a firm foundation for what lies ahead.

The repertoire of classical music and French terminology will follow them throughout their ballet experience whether as a dancer, or a member of the audience.

Not to say you can never use Disney music or music with singing, just not all the time! Please let the students keep some music that they can enjoy dancing to at home!

"Fifth positions, heads, musicality, energy. Not technical things so much – getting your leg higher or doing more turns, but things that would set you apart from other dancers. The only way you can be different is to be yourself. If you don't find your spirit and reveal it, you just look like every other dancer." - Suzanne Farrell

The traditional uniform for PreBallet students is all pink - leotards, tights, and shoes. A variation may be a black leotard, pink tights and pink shoes.

But the ballet school should have a dress code, not to be strictly enforced but gently adhered to, as an introduction to class standards.

Does this mean that I will not let a child who is not "dressed out properly" take class?

Not at all, but improper dress should not be a regular occurrence. Every effort should be made to be properly dressed for the vast majority of the classes.

Why are ballet students asked to wear the same color leotard, tights, and shoes in class?

For the visual acuity and discernment of the teacher!

When all the students are dressed the same, the teacher can see the class perform the steps better and spot problems earlier.

Corrections can be made and are easier to enforce because the teacher's field of vision is clean and uncluttered.

I have taught at studios where I felt as if I was looking through a kaleidoscope trying to pick out individual pieces of colored glass.

I can do it, but not as easily and quickly as when the class wears the same color of leotard, tights, and shoes.

A word about hair... Why must hair be arranged and pulled back in a bun?

1. To teach mothers and fathers dexterity?
2. To confound mothers and fathers indefinitely?
3. Because hair blowing into a child's eyes is a distraction?

Hair gets sweaty then sticky. Hair affects the peripheral vision of the student, loose hair may even precipitate falling or crashing into another student.

Especially in PreBallet class, a student can easily be distracted by unruly hair that is not properly secured.

Hair in a bun is the norm in ballet classes and the reason is for the safety and comfort of the students. Always.

Chapter Seven

P IS FOR PASSION, POTENTIAL, PERFORMANCE, AND PERSEVERANCE

"Great dancers are not great because of their technique; they are great because of their passion." - Martha Graham

CHILDREN DANCE ALL THE TIME — around the house, in the yard, up and down aisles in the grocery store. Parents start to think that ballet lessons might refine and direct their boundless energy.

Quite perceptive!

Dancers don't give up. Not in class. Not in performance. And certainly not in life.

Perseverance is the quality that combines strength and stamina to build endurance.

The will to continue is born from the discipline of attending class and working within the confines of your body to excel.

PreBallet parents often bring their students to take class because they see a passion for life in their young child.

Children try everything. Fly? Just give them a minute. They can do that! They'll show you!

Parents fall in love with their little ones at this age.

Why not? They can talk, are potty trained, and provide an endless source of amusement. If they can't do something or make a mistake while trying, they laugh, adorably cute and funny.

They are unspoiled and the world is open with possibility before them. Every small movement is a promise of brilliance to come.

"I don't want people who want to dance; I want people who have to dance."
- George Balanchine

When I teach PreBallet students, I experience their boundless enthusiasm and energy.

That is why my aim, and the goal of every teacher or parent of a PreBallet, should be to preserve the passion that is so captivating in that child.

Passion creates drive and drive motivates the best effort in any field of study or athletic endeavor.

This is quite a hat trick! Why?

Because training is a process that yields small triumphs over a period of time to achieve results.

The potential held within the passion of a PreBallet student must be cherished and cultivated to be revealed in performance.

What an oxymoron! That sounds completely self-evident and so stupid to say out loud!

Right?

It's not.

The balance between potential and performance in a student is judged by the quality of their movement! Because that is what ballet, dance, any athletic endeavor is... Movement.

Movement, not static poses, are the essence of every athletic endeavor, every dance step, every Olympian challenge.

Ballet training refines and directs natural energy to create neural pathways that, through repetition, increase efficiency, strength, and stamina.

The scale of potential vs. performance tips back and forth during training. I believe the scale should always favor the potential exhibited in the passion of the PreBallet student.

What do I mean?

PreBallet class should be an opportunity to explore the boundaries of human movement.

In ballet, a student does not leave or graduate from a class, whether PreBallet, Basic, or Intermediate without carrying the skills learned in that class to the next level.

If the PreBallet foundation is well grounded, all subsequent levels and the appreciation of the art form will expand from this base.

The class should never squash a student.

That's a terrible thought but I've certainly seen it often enough.

––––––––

In any profession, there are people who "play" the part: the physician who is never seen out of scrubs or a white coat; the violinist who carries their instrument like a talisman everywhere they go; the parents whose only topic of conversation is their own children.

Ballet is a natural for imposters. Hair always in a bun. So many black clothes that someone might mistake the person for a Goth. An oversize ballet bag filled with smelly shoes and an occasional Snickers bar hauled around constantly.

What I often wonder is why the person feels like such a fake that he or she needs to dress the part?

What does this add to their skill?

As a ballet instructor, I see students dance before me in every class. They wear leotards and tights but when you really get down to it, that is like wearing nothing at all.

For auditions at the Bolshoi and Mariinsky, students present in underwear – only the bottoms – yes – for boys and girls, although they are not in the same room at the same time.

Why are the students viewed in underwear? Because when a person dances, their body is on view.

But is that all?

No. Much more than that is laid bare during a performance. A person's soul is there for all to see.

———

"What's so wonderful about ballet is that it's mind-driven physicality. It's almost a Greek ideal of body, mind, and form." - Edward Villella

My main complaint about dancers in upper more advanced classes is that they are too cautious and careful.

They are too often afraid to make a mistake, or be singled out, and possibly corrected for an error.

I don't care if a student gets it wrong. I want them to dance. Be Bold! I want to see every student try their best. We can always repeat the exercise. If we bomb, let's bomb big! We will try again!

"Only children believe they are capable of everything." - Paulo Coelho

PreBallet students dance for themselves.

Teachers and parents should support and encourage all the silly awkward steps, the wild gangly arms, the attempts to place their feet in the correct position with their hands before they start dancing.

Focus on improved quality of movement, never perfection.

With PreBallet students, I search for glimpses of the finely tuned balance between potential and performance.

PreBallet parents are delighted by each small step of their student. They film all first attempts during the observation class or while they dance during participation class. If only parents had the patience and perseverance of their students...

———

The performance of a Basic level dancer is never quite as pleasing.

Parents who were once happy at every movement suddenly begin to notice deficiencies. They compare the progress of their student with other dancers in the class.

Or if the student is doing well, parents and sometimes even teachers, are tempted to prematurely push the promising student to the next level with older dancers.

If the student is more challenged and not advancing as quickly as parents think they should, the parents often request a meeting with the teacher.

Bent knees, a protruding stomach, floppy arms, difficulty remembering exercises, or a general lack of coordination during combinations become major issues.

Often, this just reflects the developmental stage of the dancer. Maybe the dancer is just on the journey to becoming the dancer they will be, but they are not there yet.

I have trained and studied ballet for most of my life. I started my dance training as a basic; switched to a ballet-only studio later; put myself through college teaching twenty ballet classes a week; danced professionally; and have taught since.

I am the person who tells Sugar Plum or Swan Queen where she is supposed to be onstage and what she is supposed to do. I coach her to pull her trailing arm in during her diagonal pique turns or point out that she is sitting in her hip during Fouettés - the 32 in a row en pointe straight kind.

I see every little flaw of every level dancer. That is my job! But...

I also know that perseverance is the goal that unites potential and passion to performance whether in ballet or life.

———

"When I was very young, I was very shy, but at the same time, I was very open because I was very curious, so I wanted to try many things."
  - Sylvie Guillem

Let your student try. At their own pace and in their own time. They may surprise you.

Remember the Ugly Duckling! They may surprise themselves. Sylvie Guillem is a prima ballerina who is legend! No one has every described her as shy!

Chapter Eight

S IS FOR SAMPLE CLASS, T IS FOR TURNOUT, AND W IS FOR WARM-UP

"Dance is your pulse, your heartbeat, your breathing. It's the rhythm of your life."

    – Jacques d'Amboise

PREBALLET CLASS WORKS BEST when the class follows a clear, simple pattern of contrasts. Upstage and Downstage. Stage Right and Stage Left. A line and a circle. Fast and Slow.

The structure of my PreBallet class has evolved over many years of observation, countless hours of teaching, and continued study with other master teachers.

I do not pretend that it is the perfect class, but the class contains elements that are effective, proven, and fun! No more and no less.

The class consists of three parts:

1. Warm Up and Stretches in the Centre Circle
2. An Abbreviated Ballet Barre
3. Studies in Opposites – Dances in the Centre

The Inclusive Circle

When my students enter class, I am already sitting in a Jump-Sit position, legs crossed, correct posture with back straight and hands folded in lap, at the centre of the classroom.

I greet each student by name then go over names again before practicing Jump-Sit.

I do not wait or hold the class past the appointed start time for anyone.

If a student arrives late, they are welcome to join the class at the point where they enter. I always welcome a child into class. It's usually not their fault that they are late.

Centre Stretches and Warm-Up

Class begins with a simple warm-up in the center. Standing in a circle, we begin by raising arms to the ceiling to try to be as tall as a giraffe, then crouching to the floor and acting as small as a mouse.

Notice I said crouching to the floor. Do not let any student get down on the floor.

The only way anyone sits in class is by performing a Jump-Sit then they must sustain correct posture and quiet hands.

No one is allowed to flop down because they are tired and have no stamina. A main goal of the class is to increase endurance and strength.

After this initial stretch, I lead the students in circling their wrists inward for eight counts then outward for another eight counts.

With arms held out to the side like a scarecrow, elbows circle next, again eight counts out and in.

Next, we make big circles with our arms at the shoulder, pretending we are pitching a softball underhand over into the parking lot.

Still within the circle, we move on to spring jumps where we jump and place our heel on the floor then jump again, crossing the same foot in a pointed position over the ankle.

On the third jump, both feet come to a parallel first position and we clap our hands.

Start this exercise off slow because it is harder to perform than it looks. Deliberately going over the combination at the beginning will help avoid falls.

When the exercise is repeated, we perform the same step, but faster.

Finally, on the third repeat, a turn is added after the foot is crossed over the ankle. I like to say that I am unscrewing my feet because that is a little what it looks and feels like.

Next, we dance a rhythm game.

Two big claps followed by three little claps. Two big jumps followed by three little jumps. All exercises are performed to eight counts on each side.

Another cadenced dance follows.

One, Two, Three, Hold the fourth count. Begin with claps, follow with jumps, and finish with spring points.

Encourage the proper toe to heel landing and takeoff on the spring points. The students will need this with every jump they take off and land during their entire career!

Every step in ballet and the trademark ballet walk always starts at the toe and rolls through the foot to the heel.

Regular street walking is heel to toe, so this is a skill that must be practiced until it becomes natural. I walk toe to heel most of the time as my regular way of movement.

Why do dancers do this? Because the toe to heel walk is what makes dancers seem to glide across the room.

In a jump, the toe is the last part of the foot to leave the floor during take-off and the first part of the foot to touch the floor when landing.

This allows for greater height and a soft, as near to silent landing for both Petit and Grande Allegro.

I can tell if a student is landing properly with my eyes closed. All I have to do is listen to the landing.

Does it sound like a jackhammer?

The toe to heel landing also goes a long way in preventing injury.

Years of slamming the heel into the floor can create some dramatic bone spurs!

Back to the exercise: three claps, jumps, and spring pointes with a hold on the fourth count.

This is one of the student's favorite exercises in the centre because this game is similar to the game of freeze.

They stop and hold whatever position occurs on the fourth count and of course, they love to come up with some pretty silly positions that they must hold absolutely still!

Freeze!

Centre warm-up work concludes with stretches on the floor. During the entire warm-up and stretch time in the centre, the students remain in a circle.

The first floor stretch is Hello Toes, Goodbye Toes. Sounds like a bedtime story!

With legs stretched parallel directly in front, we say "Hello Toes" as we flatten our feet out. Pulling our toes back and touching the tops of our toes is a good approximation of a V-sit stretch.

When we reverse and say, "Goodbye Toes," we point our entire foot away from the body.

The student should be encouraged to point the foot from their ankle, not just curl their toes, pushing their entire foot straight out as if the bones of their lower leg extend through their foot all the way to their big toe.

A sickle foot is never pretty and should be discouraged as soon as possible because the "line" of the leg should always appear straight, not broken at the ankle.

A sickle foot curves inward and away from the straight line presented by the bones of the lower leg, creating the appearance of a sickle.

The Butterfly stretch is a favorite. I always pretend that I glue the bottoms of my feet together with Gorilla Glue then immediately add a disclaimer to never to try this at home! Hold onto ankles NOT feet.

After metaphorically gluing the bottoms of our feet together, we pull our feet into our body and drop our knees as far to the side as possible.

As the exercise is performed, we concentrate on correct posture, keeping our back as straight as possible.

Why is this called a Butterfly stretch? Because we flap our turned out legs up and down which is an extension of our initial stretch.

Once the students are proficient, another added stretch can be performed from this position.

Still holding onto our ankles with our feet "glued" together and with legs bent and opened to the side, we rock back and forth then roll over onto our hip and shoulder and continue to roll until we turn 180 degrees to recover in the same Butterfly position but facing the opposite direction.

This is a great exercise for developing abdominal core strength which is usually lacking in PreBallet students. Also, it's a lot of fun to roll around on the floor. The students are much better at this than I am!

Next, we perform Y scale stretches from the Jump-Sit position.

With special attention to keeping the back straight in good posture, the seated student holds under the right foot at the heel with the right hand then extends their leg up as close as possible to the side of the head.

When the Y scale stretch is relatively stable on both sides, the students can try doing a Y scale stretch with both legs, which requires them to balance on their bottom!

Both of these exercises foster the basic ballet principal of turnout which is key to a dancer's stability and extension.

A dancer is able to balance better using turnout.

Also, because of the increased flexibility in the hip joint using a turned out leg, the dancer is able to lift their leg much higher.

Wait! What does turnout even mean?

Turnout of the leg means that instead of the leg facing straight forward as in the knee is pointing forward, the leg turns ninety degrees from the body at the hip joint.

Never force turn out from the knee or foot. Ultimately, that is impossible and dangerous.

Think of the five basic positions of ballet. In each position, the leg "turns out" from the hip which means the leg rotates in the hip joint as the heel is brought forward. The knee faces to the side although the person continues to face front.

There have been treatises written on turnout. In a perfect world, a dancer would have ninety degree turnout of each leg adding up to one hundred eighty degrees. In a perfect world...

A teacher who insists on "perfect" turnout can cause a great deal of harm.

How much turnout is enough? How much will work to produce a good dancer?

For any student from PreBallet to Advanced, the individual's natural degree of turnout should be measured and judged by the flexibility of that student's individual hip joint.

While standing in first position, heels together, legs turned out to the side, and performing a Demi-Plié, the knees should bend directly over the toes in the first position. This simple exercise is a good measure of a dancer's turnout.

If the toes are more "turned out" and the knees bend in front of the toes, then the student is forcing the turnout. Over time, a forced turnout can lead to horrific knee and foot injuries.

NEVER force turnout, especially in PreBallet!

Turnout can be improved through stretching and increased strength over a period of time but should never be strained.

Centre Warm-Up and Stretches usually take about fifteen minutes of an hour PreBallet class. Several other games and stretches can be used if time permits.

I like to pretend that I hear a lion roaring in the distance. Then we get on all fours, knees and hands, and stretch back to sit on our heels. This is similar to a Child's Pose in yoga.

Then we pretend that we are rolling a peanut across the floor with our nose as we push from this curled position up to all fours again.

While up on all fours, we stretch our back into a hump like a camel then sway our back to a hollow like an old horsey.

From all fours, I also stretch one leg parallel to the floor while lifting the opposite arm parallel to the floor.

Control of the trunk develops strength in the abdominal and back muscles while promoting balance.

All this begins in PreBallet. As you can see, we are already forming the important skills for any athletic interest as well as a healthy lifestyle.

Other stretches in the centre include activities like pantomiming animals, cats and dogs are favorites, and of course, playing the Jump-Sit game.

Every student whispers a number to me then stands in the circle. I whisper the numbers and when they hear their number, they Jump-Sit. This also helps to teach the value of listening closely and carefully.

PreBallet Barre

After our centre warm up, I stand and go to the barre. As I do this, I expect each child to remain in the circle seated in a Jump-Sit position mindful of their posture and quiet hands.

I then call each child individually by name to the barre. This is where I introduce the concept of the Ballet Run which consists of running on half-pointe with fast but quiet feet.

First, the student runs around the circle of fellow classmates then to meet me at the barre.

Are you aghast? Barre work for a PreBallet student?

Yes. A very abbreviated introduction to the ballet barre.

Because so much ballet training takes place at the barre, it is important to introduce the barre early as well as the concept of taking turns, performing the Ballet Run to the barre, keeping quiet, and being attentive as others complete their turn, all the while practicing good posture while sitting in Jump-Sit waiting for your own turn.

I have two main objectives to accomplish with a PreBallet barre. I reinforce the importance of spacing at the barre by moving from place to place as the individual student runs to join me at the barre.

I physically place them, showing each student where to stand in relation to other students already at the barre.

Proper distancing and placement from both the barre and from other students at the barre are habits that warrant practice.

You already know that bad habits are hard to break and the

students must know their spatial relationship to the barre and to others to achieve best results.

I can always tell if an older student has received credible training by how they hold the barre. That simple but telling action lets me immediately know how much retraining is necessary.

———

A friend I danced with in my early teens was invited to audition for a prestigious high school for the performing arts that, at the time, was located in Michigan.

There was no sending a video with your cellphone. A live in-person appearance was the only way to audition.

Now, New Orleans is a long way from Michigan especially before the Interstate Road system was fully completed.

My friend's mother, a wonderful lady who had never before been north of Lake Pontchartrain, drove her to the school, an epic task.

Once inside the studio, the group of six teachers asked my friend to face the barre, place two fingers on the barre and développé to second, on each side.

That was it! That's all, Folks!

Because of her strength and placement at the barre, my friend was awarded a full scholarship on the basis of an audition that lasted less than five minutes following a car ride lasting over twenty hours! Well Done!

———

Placement from the barre is initiated by arms opening from first to second position then placing the hand that is nearest to the barre on the rail, slightly in front of the body to balance.

Using the barre to hold a position that will never work in the centre is useless. A student should never jam their body right next to the barre, grabbing the barre for dear life or acting as if they are carrying a purse under their arm.

The last time I looked, barres are not allowed onstage or in the centre to facilitate dance.

If you are off balance at the barre, then you are not training to dance on balance in the centre.

Barres augment proper training and should not be used as a crutch to permit poor posture and balance.

Students often giggle as they picture a barre with tennis balls on the supports that look similar to their grandparent's walker. This is immensely helpful for the elderly, but not so practical for dancers moving to the centre or dancing onstage.

I take special care with a student's placement at the barre. No one hangs from the barre like a monkey. I know this makes for cute photos on Instagram, but the barre is not a jungle gym and should only be used to steady a student and foster balance.

My second objective with a preparatory ballet barre in PreBallet class is to familiarize students with the first two of classical ballet's five positions for both legs and arms.

————

Throughout my years of teaching, I have often seen the misuse and abuse of the five positions of classical ballet. When I moved to Houston as a professional dancer with some teaching experience at Lelia Haller's studio in New Orleans, I was poor. Yip, no other way to look at it.

My husband and I were newlyweds, and we didn't have any money since we spent it all to move to Houston, get an apartment with fleas... Whoa! That's another story!

I answered an advertisement in the Houston Chronicle for a ballet teacher.

I thought it was pretty strange to see an ad in the classifieds for a ballet teacher. I haven't seen one before or since.

The pay was not only decent but really good. Ballet teachers are usually paid a fixed price per class whether two or twenty students are in class.

Anyway, I called and arranged to meet with a middle-aged lady who offered ballet classes to children in after-school programs at established daycare centers, which was a relatively new idea at the time.

Parents paid a monthly fee on top of daycare expenditures that I learned later was equal to the monthly fees at some of the best ballet schools in the city.

For the interview, I dressed out, had my hair fixed, and brought music to demonstrate the class I would teach.

The woman lived in an upscale home within the beltway and she was pleasant enough as she met me at her front door. I followed her to an elaborate, dark den, which would definitely be called a man cave today.

She asked me to show her the five positions.

I remember looking at her as if this was a trick question.

"The five positions?" I asked.

Yes. That's all she wanted to see.

So, I went through the five positions, both arms and legs at the same time on one side and was about to continue on the other side when she stopped me with a smile. She thought I would be perfect. Hmmm...

I went with her to tour the daycare centers which were part of a giant chain. This was before there were state regulatory agencies for daycare centers and the centers were packed with kids.

Turns out, she was raking in money while claiming to teach ballet in the after-school care program. What she did was go through the five positions... That was it. Then she let everyone free dance the rest of the time.

My heart was in my throat. I asked if I could teach my regular class. Nope. I pleaded. Nope. Just the five positions and free dance for top dollar.

I declined. She would call me every couple of months to see if I would reconsider but...

Ballet's classic five positions are only a starting point. They are where we begin and certainly not an end in itself. Do I teach the five positions in PreBallet class? Nope. Only two.

This is another excellent reason why it is worth taking some time to observe a PreBallet class as a parent.

I would always be suspicious of a studio that does not allow you to observe a class before enrolling your child for instruction.

————

I teach first and second position in my PreBallet class. We perform three Demi-Plié and one relevé on each side, complete with Port de Bras, in first and second position then repeat.

The main takeaway with the Demi- Pliés which can be performed facing the barre or with one hand on the barre is that the knees bend directly over the big toe, no more, no less. Remember turnout?

The Relevé must be practiced on half-pointe. The foot has to bend. PreBallet feet are so small that the students have a tendency to go up en pointe without meaning to!

Maybe they do mean to!

But don't let them... I sometimes lightly place the bottom of my foot over the student's toes to emphasize that the foot should bend and raise only to half-pointe.

I then move to Petite Battement, as in Tendu a la second, because turnout in second is the most important and difficult to achieve.

If a Tendu can be performed in second position, then it can also be performed to fourth front and back. Since body alignment at this age is iffy at best, I use seconde as the mainstay for Tendu.

For the Tendu exercises, I use the visual imagery of standing ankle deep in mud or sand and ask the student to push down first then out through the sloughy mud or cool sand. I want the student very early to work their foot through the floor.

Finally, we finish our barre with Grande Battements.

Before Christmas, we stand with our backs to the barre to do Grande Battements to the front then face the barre to perform Grande Battements to the side. We add Battement Tendu strategically in between each high kick.

After Christmas, we face the barre standing in first position with the shoulders and hips facing the wall and try Grande Battement Derrière, a high kick to the back.

This is also a good exercise to reinforce body alignment, with shoulders and hips facing front and not turning just because you are kicking to the back.

With Grande Battements, I again emphasize tendu using the ankle deep in mud imagery then just take it higher with the big kicks.

Sometimes if the class is particularly adapt, I introduce fourth position near the end of the class year but only for Demi-Plié.

Depending on whether it is a "young" class or a class where the majority of the students will be passing to basic in the next year, I will also trace the semi-circular pattern of Ronde de Jambe, circle of the leg, and introduce the idea of en dehors (outside) and en dedans (inside) to the class.

Leading up to and including the barre, the students have been focused, under control, and precise through stretching, jumping, and barre work.

Now it's time for fun!

Centre Dances

Picture the class. For the last half an hour, the students have been warming up, jumping, stretching, trying our hand at the barre work, all the while listening closely for their name which can come at any moment with a request for a Jump-Sit or a Ballet Run.

Next as the students try not to lean on the barre, which is a no-no, and with all eyes on the teacher, what do I do?

I yawn. Not very politely, but a really big yawn.

I cover my mouth, but then I stretch both arms all the way to my fingertips and while looking at my students I say, "Gosh, I'm really tired. I'm going to take a nap."

Then I Ballet Run with fast but quiet feet to the front of the classroom and lie down on the floor with my eyes closed.

I love the reaction the first time I do this.

PreBallet students tend to take everything an adult says literally and for a moment, the entire class believes that I am sleeping on the floor at the front of the studio.

Then I open my eyes and whisper, "Aren't you tired? Don't you want to nap too?"

The whole class does a Ballet Run on fast but quiet feet, then lies down on the floor beside me. I start the music for our first dance in the centre, Asleep in a Beautiful Garden.

As the music begins, I sit up on my heels with my legs folded beneath me, but I slouch a bit and yawn again. I pretend to rub the sleep from my eyes and stretch my arms then I look from side to side.

"Oh My Gosh! Where are we?"

We are in a Beautiful Garden. I love the way PreBallet students buy into the fantasy. They tell me to watch out because they don't know who owns the garden and a troll or giant may be lurking.

I reassure them that we have been transported to a Beautiful Garden full of blooming flowers so that we can pick a bouquet for our mothers or whoever we choose!

We stand, without using our hands or arms to push ourselves from the floor to our feet, and Ballet Run yet again from stage right to stage left.

The student whose name is called gets to choose the color and type of flower for everyone to pick.

I make every effort to alternate names so everyone has a turn but that is not always possible so the next week, I have to remember who was not chosen the week before.

What I also do is call students who were not chosen for flower picking to help with another of the centre dances. It's amazing how if I make a mistake, the child who was chosen twice will fess up and suggest someone who wasn't picked.

After we gather a flower, we execute a Soutenu turn before continuing to ballet run to the opposite side of the room.

What is the purpose of running from one side of the room to another?

Well, we practice the Ballet Run on fast but quiet feet, and we learn to run together as a Corps de Ballet which is helpful and safer than running as if we are in a competitive race.

As I said previously, I never pick the first person to get to the opposite side of the room.

When we finish, we return to our circle which now surrounds a crystal clear pond and we gather water in a pretend vase then put our flowers in the vase, naming the color and type of flower.

Regrouping with a Jump-Sit to a circle gives everyone a chance to rest a moment before moving onto the next dance.

The Bunny Rabbit dance is a favorite. Again, I call students by name, and the children Ballet Run to a line upstage at the back of the room. We put our ears on, our bunny nose and tail, and two big bunny teeth. Our paws are held together right under our chin and we jump with our feet parallel but together. All this sounds very easy but consider the students are three to five years of age.

We jump twice then we take two counts to pick a vegetable in the garden, but we also look for Mr. McGregor because this is his garden!

Not such a safe garden as the flower extravaganza!

Most of the children have heard of Peter Rabbit and they know that we are wise to keep a lookout.

The jump-look sequence is repeated four times forward and four times back then we hop without stopping in a large circle to the end of the music when we Jump-Sit and of course, gobble down all the carrots, lettuce, radishes, and sometimes, a butternut squash thrown in the mix.

I hope you are beginning to recognize the pattern of the class.

Intense activity with specialized movement followed by a brief but controlled rest and reboot. There are six dances remaining. That is a lot of activity, but strength and endurance are one of the primary goals of PreBallet class.

In every succeeding level of ballet class from Basic to Advanced, there are steps and combinations of steps that require a certain strength level to accomplish, not to mention pointe work but let's not get ahead of ourselves.

An adequate strength level with a good amount of endurance contributes to any mental and physical achievement.

Many children today do not get the outside playtime physical activity of earlier generations for many different reasons.

If your child does, then good for you as a parent, but over many years of teaching, I have seen a general decline of physical strength and mental acuity in the average PreBallet age child.

Imagination and play are how a child learns to interact with the world. Many of the centre dances of my PreBallet class rely heavily on creativity and directed play.

Reality is suspended in light of much loftier goals.

When someone doesn't have the strength, both mental and physical, or the inventiveness, and ingenuity to continue, they quit, and quitting becomes a design for defeat.

Which leads to an important part of class... Attendance.

The child must attend class regularly to get anything out of the instruction.

Once or twice a month just won't cut it. Is the result worth it?? Absolutely, but you must get the child to the studio and in the class.

Sounds like a foregone conclusion. Right? Not so. If a child is not present on a regular basis, the instruction will not take root.

And attendance implies that the child is rested and ready to go. Remember that your time and money will only be well spent if your child fully engages in the lessons paid for.

Back to the Centre Dances...

The next four dances are studies in contrast. The Bee Dance and Eagle Dance both rely on the now famous, or infamous, Ballet Run with fast but quiet feet, but the difference between the two dances is the arms.

The Bee Dance uses fast but quiet feet and fast arms while the Eagle Dance uses fast but quiet feet and slow arms.

The purpose of the two dances is to allow the student to explore tempo changes and to experience moving parts of the body at different rhythms.

Sort of like patting your head and rubbing your tummy at the same time! By the way, I've never met a ballet dancer who couldn't do this!

As per usual, I call each child individually by name to the line for the Bee Dance.

But for the Eagle Dance, I arrange the lines according to age and birthday. This gives the class a chance to acknowledge a student's birthday and allow them to be leader of the line!

The Eagle Dance runs two to three concentric circles, each going in opposite directions.

You can see how this reinforces the underlying principles of corps de ballet, who may work together onstage, but do not always perform the same steps!

If you squint, you'll be able to see the triangles and circles of the Wilis in *Giselle*!

The Toy Soldier and Rag Doll dances are quite different from the other centre work.

First, there are no Ballet Runs! What! No, none at all. Both of these dances focus on smaller movements, balance, and coordination.

Let me be clear! Toy Soldiers have no knees, and they are very serious. This dance always produces the straightest lines of the class.

As I walk in back of the line to "wind" up each Toy Solider, I have been known to tickle the soldier and through great effort on the part of the dancer, I rarely get more than a suppressed giggle... Even if I really try!

Toy Soldiers are known for sharp staccato movements, first of arms bent at the elbow and moving out and away from the body then of arms and head repeating the same step together.

Toy Soldiers bow by placing their heel on the floor in front of them and bending over as far as they can. The step combines balance with a good stretch.

Toy Soldiers turn to the right then left by lifting their feet but never bending their knees. They move forward by using Grand Battements to take a step.

What happens at the end of the dance? They wind down, of course. They are just Toy Soldiers.

We do not Jump-Sit at the end of this dance but go directly into the Rag Doll dance which is a polar opposite of the Toy Soldiers.

These poor Rag Dolls must contend with missing stuffing. Their arms go limp, then their head, then their back.

Oh, My Goodness! Never fear, as they are re-stuffed, they regain some measure of fit and form. The Rag Dolls are unstuffed and stuffed two separate times.

Accentuating the smooth, fluid movement of the body as the stuffing is removed and replaced, this dance also introduces a key concept of ballet Port de Bras or "carriage of the arms."

Arms and legs should always move from the inside out. A simpler explanation might be that the dog wags his tail, the dog's tail does not wag the dog. Although if you've ever had a boxer, you may not believe my explanation.

Look at a prima ballerina's arms. The impetus of motion in her arms whether dancing Dying Swan or Giselle moves from her core through her shoulders to her elbows, wrist, hands, and finally to the tips of her fingers. Not the other way around.

The grace and poise that is naturally attributed to dancers is founded in the principle of moving the body from the inside out.

From these two relatively static dances that are nonetheless important because they speak to the way dancers move, the class will perform the most strenuous dance of the hour, the Pony dance.

Most if not all of the directed motion of the class has been centered around the fast but quiet feet of the Ballet Run but now the students will be asked to prance and gallop.

While prancing, the students practice pointing their toes. As already stated, the dancer's pointed toe should always be the last to leave the floor and the first to touch the floor.

Toe to heel is central to ballet movement and is achieved through constant training. This is not a natural thing to do.

How many of you walk toe to heel or point your toe whenever it leaves the floor?

We start off with a slow prance that is really just walking and lifting the leg at the knee with the student concentrating on pointing the foot.

When we actually prance, a jump is involved. Ideally, the dancer is in the air as the feet change places. This is the ultimate goal of all jumps in ballet!

Then we proceed to a gallop, while trying to maintain our toe to heel lead in. This process usually takes a while to learn, and will not generally be mastered till far past PreBallet.

The easiest way to gallop is to put your heel down first but eventually through training, the dancers will pass through the toe to heel landing, push forward, and take off again with their toe the last to leave the floor.

The PreBallet gallop transforms later into a ballet step known as a

Chassé, which literally means chase, because that is what it looks like, one foot chasing the other.

The Chassé is an important step because it is often used as a prelude or preparation for Grande Allegro or Big Jumps.

A word about skipping...

Skipping is a developmental milestone of coordination along with the Gallop, crawling, walking, running, and jumping.

A child usually accomplishes this task when they are between four to five years old. While this is within the age group for PreBallet, the skip is usually introduced in the Basic class which is the next level up.

The Gallop in the Pony Dance is taught as a preparation for skipping and helps the process. In PreBallet, the class should focus on achievable progress in training and not forcing developmental milestones.

By the Fini of the Pony dance, we are also approaching the end of class so although the students are pretty worn out, we proceed directly to our finishing dance.

The Baby Doll dance is a fairly stationary dance performed to a slow tempo that introduces a basic Ballet step known as the Temps lié, which teaches the transfer of weight from one foot to the other.

Remember that I ask a PreBallet student to bring a doll or stuffed animal to class.

Well, during the class, the favorite doll or stuffed toy that accompanied the child to class has been watching the student from the front of the class, usually from under the mirror. For the Baby Doll dance, each student retrieves their companion.

I always pretend to have a doll or stuffed toy in my arms and if someone forgot, then they pretend with me.

We start in first position, heels together, legs turned out to the side, and push our weight over one foot then rolling through our opposite foot, toe to heel again, we transfer our weight to the opposite foot.

After transferring our weight one additional time, we rise to half pointe and turn in an individual circle, another Soutenu turn, then repeat.

Is this what the PreBallet student is thinking as they dance? No indeed!

They are concentrating on rocking their doll or stuffed animal to sleep. The doll or stuffed animal has patiently watched as the student worked the whole class and they deserve a nap!

Finally, after repeating the entire sequence four times, the student gently places their companion on the floor and tiptoes around them in both directions from right to left and reverse.

Then the student yawns and stretches while repeating the Temps lié exercise four times before lying down beside their baby doll.

That's it!

That's the end of the class!

The PreBallet version of Révérence takes place in the spirit of appreciation that is part of the Fini of every Classical Ballet class.

The elaborate choreographed bows at the conclusion of ballet performances have their origin in the tradition of Révérence. The final Dying Swan bow in which a dancer kneels then sits on their heel then folds their entire body forward over their outstretched leg makes a first appearance at the closing Révérence of Basic class.

I then go to the exit and open the door to the reception room.

As I recognize a parent or caregiver, I call the student by name. The student uses a Ballet Run to come over to me after making sure that they bring the doll or stuffed animal.

We individually practice our curtsy or bow to each other as a sign of respect and gratitude for class before I release them to their guardians.

Wow! It's way harder for me to explain the class than dance it! But I want to give you a complete picture of a PreBallet class. Is this the only way to teach PreBallet? Yes and No.

The discussion of the class was not meant as a syllabus but a starting place for you as a parent or teacher to observe, evaluate, and judge the merits of the PreBallet class you are considering for your child or teaching your students.

Be sure to visit our website at GarageBallet.com and sign up for emails because I will post an actual class as soon as conditions improve, and I am able to film.

A suggestion for teachers... Have your musical playlist prepared and ready. Searching your phone and/or changing from one list to another are distractions that PreBallet does not need.

The attention span of PreBallet students is not the best but if the class is moving, if they are engaged as dancers, if the music is clear, rhythmic, and fun, they will remain focused and attentive the entire class.

Never underestimate a PreBallet student!

Their insight and ability to connect what they do in class to how they live their life is amazing. I expect quite a lot from my students. You should as well!

For recital, I usually have my PreBallet students perform the centre dances onstage in their regular class dress with perhaps the addition of a pink chiffon skirt and a small flower headpiece.

Why? Because they are comfortable with the dances. They know them well and if they don't, their friend does.

The centre dances usually last twenty plus minutes. This is quite a long time, but since this is usually their first experience onstage, I think it's important for them to enjoy, explore, and experiment!

At this age, no parent or teacher for that matter is worried about mistakes as long as they don't fall off the front of the stage. Mess ups are still wildly adorable!

———

I remember one student who sat and did nothing for about half the time onstage.

But when her mother whispered from the wings that she was going to buy her a Cabbage Patch doll if she danced, the child got up and did a great job with the rest of the dances.

I don't recommend bribes, as cars can be pretty expensive, but I did see it happen.

Children may cry, occasionally fall, or possibly run into each other. They lose their places and have no idea what's going on, but in the end, the audience offers hearty applause, and everyone leaves happy.

———

What I usually witness is a credible performance of young dancers who know how to execute a Ballet Run, jump as high as possible, and use the entire expanse of the stage, upstage and down and forming big circles that go in one direction then reverse.

Parents and family also love seeing their children onstage for more than a couple of minutes.

And all my helpers watch from the wings!

They do not demonstrate or hog any of the attention. They have their own dances to perform and their PreBallet charges watch them in total rapture.

Learning is a process that takes time. Sometimes that means dancing and sometimes watching, but it all sticks.

Make sure your child has the best shot at learning a tradition of physical and mental instruction proven over the centuries.

I do believe Ballet Helps Everything because it offers a mindset of focus and discipline.

What child can resist?

"When a dancer comes onstage, he is not just a blank slate that the choreographer had written on. Behind him he has all the decisions he has made in life... Each time, he has chosen, and in what he is onstage you see the result of those choices. You are looking at the person he is, and the person who, at this point, he cannot help but be... Exceptional dancers, in my experience are also exceptional people, people with an attitude toward life, a kind of quest, and an internal quality. They know who they are, and they show this to you, willingly."
- Mikhail Baryshnikov

One final caution to Teachers and Parents...

Your child is a gift not an extension of your life as a dancer or person. Enjoy and encourage them for every possible moment. They grow up awfully quick.

———

I once taught two young girls from PreBallet to Advanced Intermediate. Their moms were totally dedicated to bringing them to class, making sure their hair was perfectly done, and advocating for them with the artistic director whenever anything seemed "unfair."

One mother actually took a job as receptionist at the school and used her position to discredit other parents or students whenever possible. She looked on her position as gatekeeper and pushed her daughter to the next level before she was fully prepared.

The other mother formed a habit of observing every class her daughter participated in. Each and every one. Her position as a generous donor made it difficult for the artistic director to confront her or bar her from the class.

I never saw her verbally berate her daughter during or after class, but I did notice certain "looks" and "expressions" that were telltale.

Both the girls, on the cusp of advanced class, quit.

Was that really a surprise?

I think not, but I knew them as dancers from when they were very young. I remember big smiles! They used to love to dance. I saw their smiles fade then disappear. The pressure and fear of making a mistake stole their joy.

———

"Happy Girls are the prettiest."
  - Audrey Hepburn

Don't let your aspirations and expectations as a parent or a teacher destroy your child.

As a PreBallet student, they may exude the most potential, but they are also the most fragile. A bad experience with anything can affect their lives for years to come if not forever. Guard them well.

———

I remember another young girl who as a PreBallet student, already exhibited the incredible attributes of a complete natural. She was well built, strong yet propor-

tioned, smart, and a willing, wonderful student. A Beautiful child in every way!

A friend of mine asked if I would present a program about the history of ballet and training for the seniors of her church the week before Christmas... At first, I demurred.

The program was scheduled just after a long season of Nutcracker and the last day of regular classes before Christmas break. I was tired!

But that wasn't the real reason...

As a ballet instructor, I am not particularly comfortable wearing street clothes, standing absolutely still at the front of an auditorium, and just talking!

When I teach class, I move around and speak to subject. As a dancer, I get nervous talking in front of people. My friend wouldn't take no for an answer, so I decided to request backup.

I asked this particular PreBallet student, one of my Basic students, and my youngest daughter, an advanced dancer, to come with me and act as demonstrators.

What a beautiful trio! Each dancer was the perfect example of their class and level!

I ended up enjoying the presentation. No one in the audience was looking at me at all. They were all focused on the dancers, as they well should have been.

The students were an incredible "show and tell" of how in the span of a few short years, young dancers progress from PreBallet spring pointes to Gargouillade, a jump combining a pas de chat with a double ronde de jambe. How a heel-toe-turn becomes multiple pirouettes. How jumps and claps develop into changements and entrechat quatres!

The day was clear, crisp early winter with a bright, blue sky and brilliant sunshine streaming through the windows in what had been the first assembly building of the church.

Our presentation was well received. Some of the audience even asked the girls for autographs which they thought was pretty funny since they only demonstrated a few steps from barre work and several examples from centre. They were even given bouquets of red and white carnations garnished with sprigs of evergreen!

The little PreBallet student had been dropped off at the studio where we all gathered prior to the demonstration. I invited her mom to the program, but she had to go back to work.

Later, I was quite happy when I saw her mom quietly enter the auditorium at the halfway mark.

Afterward, we all went out to a Chinese restaurant then to the bakery shop for cookies and hot chocolate, coffee for the adults. Good gracious! Dancers can eat when given the opportunity! The afternoon was golden. Perfect in every way.

The week after Christmas, the young girl's mom approached me after class. I thought she was going to comment about the program.

I was completely floored when she told me that her daughter, my promising young student, had been diagnosed with childhood cancer.

The mom said that her daughter's wish was to continue to take class as long as possible, and when she could no longer take class, she wanted to observe.

She did both.

Bravely and with a depth that was way beyond her five years. She was still beautiful in her wheelchair and she bestowed her strength and the will to do her best upon her PreBallet class and the more advanced classes that she observed as well.

At the time, I had no idea that the presentation at the church would be her first and last performance.

What is my point? What do I want to leave you with? Enjoy each moment with your PreBallet student but ensure that the instruction they receive is purposeful, playful, and professional. PreBallet is never a throwaway class...

"The world of dance is a charmed place. Some people like to inhabit it, others to behold it; either way it is rewarding." - Margot Fonteyn

AFTERWORD

Thank you for reading The ABC's of PreBallet - The Essential Ballet Building Block, the third book in the Garage Ballet series.

I hope you enjoyed the book. If you can spare a moment, please share your positive review on Amazon.

https://tinyurl.com/yy6wjdsd

Many Thanks!

ABOUT THE AUTHOR

A native of New Orleans, I studied with Lelia Haller, danced with Houston Ballet under James Clouser and Nicholas Polejenko, and have taught ballet throughout the southeast for over forty years.

I appreciate all my students and have a special place in my heart for PreBallet.

The ABC's of PreBallet – The Essential Ballet Building Block is the third book of my *Garage Ballet* series. I hope that my support and practical direction enrich your experience as a student, ballet parent, and teacher. Thank you for including Garage Ballet in your dance journey!

ALSO BY DAWN C CROUCH

Made in United States
Orlando, FL
02 October 2024

52226748R00049